Build Your Resilience in 10 Steps

A Beginner's Guide to Become Mentally Stronger, Cope Better with Anxieties and Remain Positive When Life Gets Hard

INESSA SCOTT

ISBN: 979-8-5860-6215-4

CONTENTS

INTRODUCTION

"Life doesn't get easier or more forgiving; we get stronger and more resilient."– Steve Maraboli

Everyone experiences a phase in their life where they believe the entire universe is conspiring against them. While it is just "one of those days" in the universe's books, it feels like a century of bad luck and suffering. You spilled coffee on your favorite dress, your kids are mean to you, your boss didn't approve your project, and your friends don't seem to have time for you. Minor setbacks like these can ruin any person's day. However, sulking over such mishaps and victimizing yourself for days to come is unacceptable. It is a sign of low resilience. You cannot cope with the challenges in your life, which can ruin your mood and even make you anxious.

If you undergo major incidents such as getting in a car accident or losing a loved one, it can be a genuine struggle to adapt and bounce back. It is a relief to know that everyone struggles with these issues; you are not alone.

People with low resilience may even consider constructive criticism as downgrading and discouraging. If you find yourself moping over negative feedback from your manager or sitting in despair when receiving a crude comment, you must build your resilience. While you cannot foresee all the challenges and adverse outcomes that life throws at you, you can undoubtedly mold yourself into a stronger individual and overcome such obstacles.

Although resilience has been touted as the ability to rebound from a challenge, you need inner strength to harness its power. Most of us wish to build resilience to endure tough times with ease but fail even to try. This book will teach you the true meaning of resilience and provide practical ways to become more resilient. You will also learn how to deal with low resilience and overcome every obstacle and curveball thrown your way, whether in your personal or professional life.

Read on to find out more.

CHAPTER 1

THE BASIS OF RESILIENCE

"Resilience is very different than being numb. Resilience means you experience, you feel, you fail, you hurt. You fall. But, you keep going."– Yasmin Mogahed

Before we learn how to overcome difficult situations by building resilience, let's first understand the meaning of the term resilience.

Resilience is the ability to come back stronger from inevitable disappointments and challenging circumstances. Let's take a few examples to grasp the concept clearly. A car without shock absorbers will provide an unpleasant and painful ride until you reach your destination. In reality, the car ride is your life journey, and the shock absorbers are your resilience. You need it to be happy and carefree. You can also find resilience in nature; during winter, tree branches bend to shrug off the weight of snow, thereby counterbalancing their own weight. Nature's architecture triggers the tree branches to be resilient and continue thriving despite the surrounding conditions.

Fragility is a common characteristic in most humans. If you are fragile, every little thing will upset you. You will spend your time being hurt, angry, or even depressed, which will eventually affect your relationships, productivity, work, and physical and mental health.

Resilience stems from strong willpower and a steady mindset. Once you set your mind to attaining a goal, you fulfill it by all means, which is also the secret behind building resilience. Simply put, resilience is bouncing back and coping with challenging situations. When things go wrong, you must hold your head high and stand up for yourself.

The Importance of Resilience

Before you learn how to build it, understanding the correct definition and importance of resilience can lead to a better life. As the famous quote from the movie Forrest Gump goes, "Life is like a box of chocolates, you never know what you're gonna get." You will face adversity, twists, and unexpected turns in your life. If you are thoroughly prepared to face them, you will always bounce back and help others get on their feet, too. You will be a positive influence on those who struggle to be resilient and overcome their own challenges.

To begin with, you must know that life is not always fair and just to everyone. To keep your boat sailing, you must prepare yourself and become resilient. While being hurt and depressed are natural human reflexes to any adverse situation, staying in this condition for long is often counterproductive. You are not only affecting your physical and mental well-being but also spreading negative vibes around you.

The absence of resilience also affects your productivity. It engulfs you in a downward spiral that can take a toll on every aspect of your life. If you have experienced a crushing, life-changing incident, you will need help to recover. That said, being upset over minor disappointing situations for a long time must also be resolved. If you are resilient, it will be easier for you to resume your daily life without getting overly affected. In a way, by building resilience, you are designing a roadmap to adapt to the obstacles that life throws at you. It means that you will not only dodge those curveballs on your way, but you'll also be prepared to face those that lie ahead.

Resilience is about framing your mind and soul to emerge stronger from situations that would have otherwise been too difficult to handle. In today's fast-paced and straightforward human approach, resilience can be deemed a necessity or a survival instinct to lead a fulfilling life. While reflecting on negative experiences and learning from them is essential, getting upset for days on end can affect your work and keep you from achieving your goals. Building resilience is necessary to develop self-confidence and self-esteem, which are core virtues in today's competitive world.

Going through tough times is like a hidden blessing, as it shapes you into a stronger and braver person. A resilient person is focused, positive, successful, and, most importantly, happy.

The Science of Resilience

Your body can organize its systems and achieve an equilibrium, which also applies to resilience. For instance, your body temperature is 98 degrees on average, which can change according to weather conditions and internal function. If the temperature rises, you start sweating; if it gets too cold, you begin to shiver. Your body copes with external changes and finds a way to bring it back to a state of equilibrium. All your body systems are equipped to maintain balance, which is why they are known as self-organizing systems.

Just like nature has its way of surviving in harsh weather, and your body finds a way to retain its physical functions, your mind should also learn to cope with adverse situations to achieve inner peace. It is a person's characteristics and the environment they were brought up in form an interdependent process that defines true resilience. In other words, positive aspects such as loving parents, supportive friends, and a satisfactory lifestyle work to counterbalance certain negative plights such as minor accidents or financial mishaps. This balance is true resilience.

Imagine a scale with a fulcrum loaded with experiences of good and bad things on either side. The fulcrum's main point, which also balances the scale, can be compared to our genes. These genes may make us more sensitive to negative situations or force us to look at the positive outcome. The former could be a result of parental neglect or mistreatment at an early age. Depending on the scale's alignment, the person may or may not face difficulties in coping with adverse circumstances.

It is known that experiences move the fulcrum, representing a person's ability to cope with both negative and positive situations. Some negative experiences include poverty, violence, mental illness, or poor education. In this case, the fulcrum moves away, and you become a victim of many predicaments. By contrast, if you face positive outcomes such as supporting relationships, happiness, good health, and safety throughout your life, your genes will respond accordingly. Your genes are the expression of chemical interactions; they turn up or down and govern the circuits of your brain. This, in turn, will determine the way your mind and body respond to anxiety, symptoms of depression, stress, and other mental health afflictions.

When people are taught coping skills, including behavior regulation, practical problem solving, stress management, planning, and other techniques that help manage stress, the fulcrum shifts and tilts towards positive outcomes. The science behind resilience suggests that a person's experiences throughout childhood are responsible for the way they cope with negative plights in life. Particularly if you have had a troublesome childhood, it is essential for you to learn how to build resilience to lead a gratifying and satisfying life.

CHAPTER 2

CHALLENGES TO ACQUIRING RESILIENCE

"When one door of happiness closes, another opens; but often we look so long at the closed door that we do not see the one which has been opened for us." – Helen Keller

Developing resilience is easier said than done. While remaining positive and having a better outlook on life helps you overcome disappointing experiences, practicing a positive attitude is not everyone's cup of tea. Building and practicing resilience can be a challenge in itself, which several factors can make difficult.

Why is it a Struggle to be Resilient and Stay Positive After a Setback?

Humans are wired to feel pain, fear, happiness, and a broad spectrum of feelings depending on their situation. In case a person hurts you by being rude, it is natural to feel bad and upset. It is easy to crumble; however, it isn't the end of the world. You must know that any individual who makes rude comments or hurts others is usually going through their own ordeal. It is a way of coping with their own predicament and grief. While it is not acceptable socially, you must not take it personally.

Nevertheless, it can be hard to stay positive because of several factors governed by your mindset, reality, and current situation. We are all victims of the overbearing consensus that resilience is a must-have to survive. While it is true, some individuals feel overwhelmed when they find themselves unable to build even a small fraction of resilience. In truth, it is this same pressure that keeps them from developing and practicing resilience. It would help if you had lots of courage and strength to face painful situations, which is not an easy feat. The lack of an obvious solution in front of you will increase your stress, and you will eventually start losing faith. That gut feeling that nags you to keep moving in the absence of a solution seems hopeless.

We Are Being Thrown Off Balance

Every person's struggles and ordeals vary. Furthermore, the way they are affected by a comparable situation also varies. Some cope with unfavorable circumstances by projecting the blame on those around them, whereas others suffer in silence and accumulate anger and frustration. It can lead to self-doubt, depression, and even self-harm in extreme cases. Physical symptoms may also arise, such as insomnia, hair fall, skin conditions, weight loss, or gain. One of the main culprits is stress, commonly observed in most individuals today, from young teens to seniors.

All these circumstances occur because of the inability to build and practice resilience. You are thrown off balance, and it seems challenging to bounce back from the situation. It may start with anger, followed by vengeful behavior, and lead to the destruction of precious relationships and the failure to achieve your goals. To renew, recover, and move forward, you must cultivate certain proactive behaviors, which are usually inhibited by self-doubt and a lack of personal confidence. The situation can worsen if the individual is unaware that they are indeed out of balance; you cannot treat a problem if you are unaware of the issue in the first place. Acknowledging your problem is the first step to regaining balance, which relates to self-awareness. We will discuss the importance of being self-aware to build resilience late on.

One must have the courage to confront painful realities, irrespective of how hard it can be. It may be even more difficult to keep faith that there will be a solution soon when there isn't one right away. What drives that hope? If you are not ready to change your mindset, it is challenging to cling on to the hope of finding a solution on your own. The strength to carry on despite feelings of hopelessness is burdensome.

So, how does this imbalance manifest in people? The leading cause is the inability to take responsibility, especially if you are endorsing many at the same time. We all are exposed to a never-ending rat race that can feel overwhelming at times. Juggling between studies, work, children, self-care, home maintenance, etc., is tough. Most of us do it endlessly and get stuck in a loop. We do not have enough time to rest or focus on ourselves, which may cause an imbalance. Simultaneously, failing to craft your definition of balance can make it even more difficult to achieve. A lack of self-discipline and consistency, the inability to focus on your goals, and lack of self-care can also explain the imbalance.

We Have Negative Biases

Psychologists have observed a tendency in people to process bad events more carefully than good events. The focus is shifted to the negative repercussions rather than on the positive outcomes. In a way, people believe that their happiness will be 'stolen' if they feel a gush of excitement or if things go well for too long. Most of us also think that our abilities are innate and that we are incapable of change. It keeps people from developing a growth mindset, one of the main reasons to remain stuck in life.

The capacity to embrace change and lead your life with fluid skills versus living with a set of fixed skills marks the presence of a growth mindset. Individuals with a growth mindset can endure difficult situations and challenges far more readily than those with a fixed mindset. The latter degrade themselves by comparing themselves to others, thereby accentuating the negative downward spiral. It keeps them from solving their problems and amplifies their existing issues, which leads to further stress.

Sentences like, "Maybe I am just not capable enough to finish this task," "I don't think I can ever get closer to my goals," or "I am not worthy enough to represent my company" are self-deprecating. You are insulting your own self, which further undermines your self-worth. All this is because of a negative bias that we project towards ourselves and our skills. If you find yourself in such a situation, you can turn it around by adopting a more optimistic mindset, which, as we've seen, is a challenge of its own.

In the upcoming chapters, we will explore effective ways to change your mindset to develop resilience and pave the way towards a more rewarding life.

CHAPTER 3

DEALING WITH LOW RESILIENCE

"Although the world is full of suffering, it is also full of the overcoming of it." – Helen Keller

Now that you are aware of the challenges that can act as a blockade in building resilience, you must learn the correct way to acknowledge and deal with low resilience. As mentioned earlier, most people are born with resilience as a trait that may fluctuate according to circumstances or trauma that one may face in life. Knowing the common signs that represent low resilience and deciphering your current level will help you become more self-aware and improve your reaction to resilience.

It is essential to know that emotional ups and downs will be a part of life and that the feelings of embarrassment that follow are also natural. However, if you cannot bounce back from stressful situations, your resilience may erode over time. In case you become a victim of a traumatic event or succumb to long-term stress or anxiety, your resilience level may drop at an even faster pace. If that is the case, you will know whether you need extra time for activities and mental exercises that boost resilience.

How Do You Know When You are Low in Resilience?

Certain signs can show that a person is suffering from low resilience, some of which include:

Recurring Negative Feelings

Feelings of anger, frustration, irritability, and always feeling on edge are apparent signs of the inability to develop resilience or low resilience. If you feel angry, frustrated, or want to pick up a fight over petty issues, it is time to change your behavior by working on your resilience. You will find yourself arguing over subjective matters and getting into arguments without hesitation. Developing your strength will make you more patient and make it easier for you to listen to others before presenting your opinions.

Mental Health Issues

You may also suffer from bouts of anxiety, sulking, or feeling overwhelmed. During such situations, you can get easily depressed, cry a lot, or overthink every one of your sentences or interactions. If the condition worsens, you may experience anxiety attacks with constant sweating, pulsating heart rate, dilating pupils, and extreme confusion for a couple of seconds or minutes at a time. In some cases, the effects might last longer and cause permanent damage.

Moodiness

With a lack of inspiration and low resilience, you will also witness a fluctuation in your hormonal levels, which can affect your physical health. You may get emotional over minor issues or experience random mood swings, an unwanted but apparent side effect. The inability to control your emotions may get in your way and affect your mental health because of the highs and lows you face throughout the day. It can be quite tricky to cope with such fluctuating emotions.

Getting Sick

Persistent illness is also a sign of low resilience. Do you suffer from headaches, digestive issues, or any weakness in general? It's due to the inability to cope with the negative consequences that have affected your physical health. Your immune health gets depleted because of depression, solitude, and poor eating patterns. It becomes difficult to fight the bacteria, viruses, or other harmful pathogens that attack our bodies and immune systems. Once you successfully build your resilience, you will become less prone to getting sick.

Feeling Uninspired

Losing interest in previous activities or feeling unmotivated are other clear signs of low resilience. If you have lacked the will to work or create things you were usually interested in or good at, you must build resilience. Being unmotivated can take a toll on your productivity, eventually affecting your career goals and professional success.

Trouble Sleeping

People with low resilience often experience troubled sleep. Irregular sleeping patterns, or insomnia in extreme cases, can affect your physical and mental well-being. Whenever you feel stressed or eat poorly, you cannot rest properly; and if it is a recurring pattern, it can cause health issues down the line. When minor incidents affect you in life, you tend to overthink when on low resilience. It can keep you up all night. Instead of enhancing their resilience, most individuals find solutions to fix their sleeping patterns with pills and medication. However, by working on their resilience, they can improve their sleeping pattern and prevent related issues. Once your resilience is high, you will sleep better.

Poor Memory

The inability to think or fuzzy thinking is an added effect of low resilience. When you face a setback, it is natural to feel overwhelmed at first. That said, it is easier for people with low resilience to get mixed and confused. For them, the situations they face are often a puzzle with no plausible way out. It can lead to poor memory, fuzzy thinking, and the inability to decipher and plan their thoughts.

Overreaction to Normal Situations

If any normal situation that can be overlooked makes you angry, frustrated, or triggers an overreaction, you are most likely low in resilience. For instance, if a person cutting the line at a coffee shop angers you to the point of picking up a fight with them, you will overreact to normal situations. In extreme cases, you may even fight or feel sad once you are alone. Crying over situations beyond your control is also a clear sign of low resilience.

Complete Isolation or Being Overly Dependent

Becoming isolated or making excuses not to see others can be another telltale sign. By contrast, your dependency on others may increase, which can make you over-clingy. The way you behave with low resilience depends on your nature. For example, if you are an introvert, you may shut yourself off completely and not see others for a long time. If you do not feel like meeting people (even your best friends), it is a clear sign of low resilience. It may be because of a lack of self-confidence or not being able, or wanting, to face your weaknesses.

In such situations, most people hate to socialize and make new friends. They keep themselves enclosed in a room and avoid greeting visitors, too. As a professional, networking and building new contacts is of utmost importance. Now, by isolating yourself from the world, you are not only jeopardizing your professional life but also letting go of the chance to develop your resilience.

As mentioned, extroverts who suffer from low resilience may cling on to their relatives and friends to keep going. Naturally, this behavior is unwelcome and affects personal relationships. Losing valuable relationships because of low personal resilience is irreversible, more often than not.

Reckless Behavior

Having low resilience can trigger reckless behavior such as excessive drinking, taking major steps in relationships without a second thought, uncalculated moves, spending without a limit, or the inability to get a hold of yourself in social settings. While some people do receive help, not all are lucky to be redirected on the right path.

Lack of Hope

As established, being resilient involves holding on to the hope of finding solutions soon. You can only achieve this if you hold faith. However, if you think the future is entirely hopeless, you will automatically be on low resilience. When you lack vision, developing problem-solving issues can also be a side effect. It leads to poor decision-making, which can turn into cynicism. People also perceive it as the inability to care for others, a lack of empathy.

Questioning Your Faith or Religion

At times, you may even take it to a deeper spiritual level. Most religious people believe in a higher power or a deity who answers their prayers, reassuring them, and guiding them in the right direction. However, they may start questioning or losing their faith during hard times, especially when they cannot see a tangible solution to their ordeals. Sometimes, even most religious people can end up abandoning their faith entirely.

Dwelling on Problems

Recalling your past and dwelling on issues can cause unnecessary stress. You spend too much time thinking about the challenges and issues you face rather than trying to find a plausible solution and move forward. It is known as dwelling on your problems. You might spend sleepless nights worrying about your issues and even thinking about the problems that are yet to come. Even if you are handling your problems to some extent, you may worry more than required. It is primarily because most of us filter out our experiences based on specific issues that we believe exist, irrespective of whether they actually exist. It is about censoring 'unimportant' aspects that do not support the problem. Ultimately, the only effective way to resolve this is by building your resilience.

Feeling Victimized

You may feel that the people around you are questioning your choices or picking on you, which will make you the victim. One of the primary reasons for this is the emotional distress that follows. For instance, a student's worst nightmare is getting poor grades despite studying hard; the main reason students feel pressured in the first place. This emotional fragility is felt even before receiving their grades, and it can be quite distressing. Eventually, this fragility turns into a fear of performing poorly, causing students to break down because of the stress and pressure they are experiencing. It affects their performance in the long run and results in a lack of self-confidence and self-esteem. Let's not forget the level of competition and rat-race we all are subjected to nowadays, which only adds to the emotional crises.

Emotional Eating Pattern

Binging on unhealthy foods such as chips, cookies, and chocolates when you feel stressed or angry can affect your physical, mental, and emotional health in negative ways. Binge or emotional eating is often a passive-aggressive mechanism to deal with everyday stress, at school, on the job, or even in the household or in romantic relationships. You are hurting your own body and mind by developing unhealthy eating patterns. Finishing a pack of chips or a pint of ice cream in one seating may surely distract your brain and make you forget about your issues, but it will cause you to adopt a harmful pattern that will be extremely difficult to combat in the long run. You must find a permanent fix to this short-term solution, which is at its core, is a systemic issue.

Inability to Handle Routine Tasks

Keeping up with everyday tasks such as cooking, exercising, or organizing can be difficult with low resilience. At times, you may even delay tasks, resulting in procrastination and an overall lack of productivity. When you cannot complete the tasks on your to-do list, you grow more stressed, which only amplifies the existing problem.

Although some of these signs may not seem to relate to resilience, they interconnect somehow. If you notice these signals for a prolonged period, say over six months, it is wiser to seek medical help as it could show depression. If one of these signs hinders your productivity or normal functioning over time, you must take action. Other problematic signs include the inability to deal with failure, shifting the blame to others, and lacking initiative.

Not everyone can decipher these signs by themselves. If that is the case, ask a friend or trusted support to help you identify any out-of-the-ordinary behaviors. Once you can interpret these signs by yourself, you can help others and influence people to build resilience and lead a more gratifying life.

Preparing Ahead of Time

Practically, you only discover your strength by enduring and overcoming tough times. You can build yourself up in advance and ready yourself to stay strong in the face of adversity. As mentioned, the first step is to identify the signs discussed above. Next, you must test your strength to undergo resilience-building activities.

We do not know whether the strategies to build our resilience actually work until our strength gets tested. Since the level of resilience changes according to the context and environment an individual grows in, we must shift our focus on building strength rather than pondering trauma and stress's adverse outcomes. This shift will ensure that every individual overcomes a negative outcome with a positive attitude, irrespective of the traumatic effect that they go through. Psychologists and specialized clinicians are designing more and more strength-based models to help people outgrow their low resilience.

We need to remain flexible to adjust our strategies under challenging circumstances. While designated strategies work for certain situations, you must be ready to fine-tune your approach. The goal is to build resilience and avert stressful situations.

CHAPTER 4

10 EFFECTIVE STEPS TO BUILD RESILIENCE

"Resilience is knowing that you are the only one that has the power and the responsibility to pick yourself up." – Mary Holloway

It is wise to think of resilience as a process and not a quick fix; you must take resilience one step at a time. It is a lesson to be learned throughout your entire journey. This chapter will discuss ten practical steps to build resilience and get acquainted with your old resilient self again. Once you convert these steps into a routine, be ready to witness a formidable change in your life.

Even though we often perceive resilience as extraordinary, in reality, it is a common trait that most people possess. A lack of resilience is only because of situational circumstances, trauma, or temporary emotional pain. You always carry a part of resilience with you; it might be hidden due to distress.

Nevertheless, you can rebuild or unleash it by implementing specific changes and effective strategies proven successful. You must also know that resilience is never a constant; the mindset of 'being born with it' is not entirely correct. Even if you lack resilience, you can always develop it along the way. By working on your thoughts, feelings, behaviors, and actions, you can minimize distress and reap the positive effects of a strong resilience.

Implement the following steps to build your resilience over time:

Step 1: Develop Self-Awareness

Self-awareness is key to developing resilience. By knowing yourself inside out, you can outline your strengths and weaknesses and use them to your advantage. While using your strengths is undoubtedly important, you must also learn to navigate your weaknesses to showcase the best version of yourself and fulfill your goals. It also helps you take conscious actions and rebalance your foothold by allowing you to preach competent practices, regain your prowess, and channel your energy in the right direction.

At times, you will typically respond to stress and adversity in an ill-suited manner. Let's say you had a hectic day at work, and you cannot wait to drive back home and relax. Upon reaching your place, you find a messy house with your kids shouting and fighting with each other. Instead of coping with the stressful situation adaptively, you drive yourself to a local bar and turn off your cellphone to enjoy a well-deserved drink in peace. It is an ill-suited way of coping with an unwanted situation. To resolve this, you must learn specific adaptive strategies. Failing to do so can worsen the situation and foster hidden anxiety and stress.

So, how can one develop self-awareness?

- The first move is to understand your strengths and weaknesses. Learn your stress triggers and pay attention to them, as this acknowledgment will eventually pave the way for viable solutions.

- Practice emotional distancing from challenges and negative people. If you are the target of harassment, bullying, or jokes in public gatherings, emotional detachment is of the utmost importance. It will keep you from constant anxiety, unwanted drama, and stress.

- Stop being a victim and take responsibility. Nothing in this world can affect you unless you let it. For this, you must stop blaming others for the troubles you have to endure, as this is a powerful sign of hopelessness. In short, act like a survivor instead of a victim. As the famous lines from Maxine Schnall's book What Doesn't Kill You Makes You Stronger, "A victim asks how long it will take to feel good — a survivor decides to feel good even if things are not so great" and "A victim focuses on pain of loss — a survivor cherishes remembered joy."

- Re-evaluate the meaning of your life. Ask questions like, "What is your life's true purpose?" "What are your goals?" and "What do you want to achieve in life that will define your purpose?". If you cannot find definite answers to these questions, you will keep wandering forward, which can make you susceptible to life's adversities. Your life should not be mundane, and you must seek excitement and seize opportunities at every turn. It will nurture self-awareness.

- It would help if you also accepted that some situations are beyond your control. While you may be fully prepared to face adversities and withstand shortcomings, do not feel defeated if you cannot be in charge all the time.

- Give yourself time to grieve and embrace your feelings, especially if you are going through a difficult phase. You must know that it is all right to feel sad and anxious when things get tough. Unless you are not willing to bounce back, or even try to, acknowledging your grief is critical.

Being self-aware will not only help you build your resilience, but it will also encourage people to respect and admire you. In a way, practicing self-awareness means unleashing your authentic self to the world, which most people admire. It will enhance your personality and allow you to build your confidence, as well.

Step 2: Build Self-Regulation Skills

Knowing how to manage your feelings is of the essence, as it helps you stay afloat instead of drowning in your own emotions. Self-regulation keeps you aligned with your feelings and the actions that follow.

Use Stress-Reduction Techniques: These will help you regulate your emotions, thoughts, and behaviors without feeling constrained. Some useful techniques include visualization practice, yoga, focused breathing, aromatherapy, massage therapy, and taking some time out of your busy schedule.

Guided Imagery: As the name suggests, this technique lets you practice mindfulness and ease stress by evoking interesting images in your mind and memory. These images convey deep meaning and reflect your life. You may need help from a practitioner to powerfully visualize and recreate sensory feelings such as taste, sound, and sight.

To practice it at home, find a quiet corner, and lay on the floor with your eyes closed. Focus on your breathing, clear your mind, and let go of your thoughts. Play calming music to promote concentration. Choose a place you like to visit; it can be in the middle of the woods or by the calm seashore on a favorite beach, anywhere that makes you happy. Imagine yourself being in that place and visualize the surrounding elements. Try to imagine the feel of the breeze on your cheeks and the smell of the flowers in the forest.

Practice this visualization technique with unique elements around you for 10 to 15 minutes. Once you open your eyes, you will feel at ease and stress-free. Practice every day to amplify the effects.

Breathing Exercise: Meditation and breathing exercises are also effective ways to reduce stress and control your emotions. Sit on the floor in a cross-legged position and place your hands in your lap. Make sure that the room is silent and calm. Close your eyes and focus on your breathing. Do not let any thoughts pour in. Let your mind stay empty and focus on your breathing. Inhale while counting to three, hold it for 3 to 5 seconds, and exhale. Repeat multiple times. For an added effect, play calming music.

Practice it daily for 10 to 15 minutes after waking up and before going to bed. Breathing exercises will help you reduce stress, control your behavior, and foster better focus and productivity.

Mindfulness Training: Mindfulness is being aware of your body, mind, soul, and existence as a whole. Being mindful works to reduce stress, repel negativity, and calm your mind. While we primarily use breathing techniques and yoga in mindfulness training, we also consider certain basic practices such as accepting yourself and living in the moment a part of this technique. Simple activities such as breathing, walking, or stretching can promote mindful thinking. When walking, pay attention to your stride; similarly, focus on the bites of food you take while eating. By staying aware and being in the moment, you will be thankful to the universe for your existence, helping develop self-love, empathy, and compassion.

Stress Reduction in Daily Activities: Performing daily activities can also be therapeutic if you program your mind towards that aim. While some consider cooking a therapeutic activity, others may view it as an obligation. However, with the right mindset, you can engage your senses and activate memories related to the activity in question. Light a candle and play some of your favorite music when you are in the kitchen. Think about what you would do in a similar situation to reduce stress while watching movies or taking a shower. Small instances like these can be the ultimate stress busters.

Step 3: Learn Coping Skills

Several coping skills that help deal with stressful and challenging situations can be applied and practiced regularly. These include:

Journaling: This practice is an effective way to keep your thoughts organized, stimulate your brain, and acknowledge your feelings. You are bound to learn more about your strengths and weaknesses by writing them down in a journal. Add colors, stickers, and other decorative elements to make it more personal and exciting. If possible, jot down your thoughts before you sleep, as it will help you recall your achievements and failures of the day in the long run. You will also gain the confidence to endure a similar situation in the future. By reframing your negative and upsetting thoughts, you will gain a positive outlook on life and learn to navigate your weaknesses in your favor.

Exercising: Getting active will not only enhance your physical health and ward off illnesses, but it also works as a coping mechanism to rebuild resilience. It will help you get through challenging times while building your confidence and physique. Exercise for at least 30 minutes daily, regardless of the intensity you choose. Activities such as walking, running, swimming, playing a sport, or dancing, can increase heart rate and improve your health over time. If you do not like exercising, pick a team sport or an activity you enjoy and get your heart pumping.

Spending Time Outdoors: Spend some time outside and get close to nature. Explore unknown places in your vicinity, take a bike ride, go hiking, or camping. It will be a coping mechanism to stress and help you reconnect with your family and loved ones. Being outdoors will enhance your self-awareness and clear your mind. You can reconnect with your authentic self and think more effectively about getting closer to your goals. Moreover, being outdoors will also benefit your physical and mental health; breathing in the fresh air and walking on natural terrain are health boosters, which you must experience regularly.

Socializing: Being around people and making connections can be quite uplifting, especially if you surround yourself with influential ones. Join book clubs or attend social events inside your professional field to meet experts from whom you can learn. While socializing is essential, you must eliminate the toxic and negative people that hinder your mental health. It would be best if you had more positive people in your life that can steer you in the right direction and help you build your self-confidence.

Get Enough Sleep: Most adults overlook the importance of sleep, which can threaten your health in the long run. In fact, an irregular sleeping pattern can cause many health issues such as weight gain, increase in stress levels, hair fall, energy depletion, and a dip in resilience. Get at least 7 to 8 hours of quality rest every night. Turn off your electronic devices at least a half-hour before bedtime, sip on some sleep-inducing herbal tea, and play relaxing music to get sound sleep.

Tap into Creative Activities: Make some time for what you love to do. It can be reading, painting, baking, dancing, or any other creative hobby that gets your creative juices flowing. These act as an escape from reality and help reduce stress significantly. Tapping into your passion is a healthy distraction from whatever predicament you may be going through, which helps you find lost faith and inspiration over time.

Avoid Media Overconsumption: Constant exposure to news outlets and social media platforms can be nerve-wracking and promote chronic anxiety. Media outlets will often sensationalize or exaggerate a piece of news to gain more viewership, which leads to fear-mongering among viewers. Shut every access to news media and social networks for at least a few hours every day. If possible, go on a social media detox for a day or more.

Create a Collection of Inspiring Images or Quotes: This will help you stay calm and positive during tough situations. Collect images and quotes from your role model or influential figures and stick them at a visible spot such as your refrigerator or bedroom door. You may also put together a vision board; this visualization technique will help you get closer to your goals and keep you hopeful during hard times and after unexpected losses.

Step 4: Increase Optimism

You will have noticed that the importance of staying positive and optimistic is repeated throughout the book. Staying positive is the secret mantra of building resilience.

Remember these key points to cultivate optimism as a character trait:

- Believe in your ability to handle challenging situations. There is nothing that you cannot overcome.

- Remember that challenges, setbacks, and difficulties will

eventually pass. If you have been through a lot, believe that better days are coming.

- Find the silver linings and tidbits that make you happy. If you cannot, create happiness by being kind to a stranger or complimenting someone. By making someone's day, you will experience joy, too.

- Focus on the positive in every situation. No matter how clichéd this may sound, you must believe that everything happens for a reason. Seeing the positive aspects in every negative situation will help you endure it with ease and keep you happy during tough times.

Now, how do you train your brain to see the bright side? How do you apply the 'glass-half-empty, half-full' theory in actual life? You begin by questioning yourself and setting an intention. Why do you want to become optimistic? Why do you feel this sudden urge to shift your mindset? Setting your intention is giving yourself a positive affirmation and writing it down.

Sentences like "I am optimistic" and "I am doing my best to be more positive" will aid in intention setting. Next, pick five things that make you happy and induce positivity. It can be your pet, your achievements, or supportive members in your entourage. Write them down in the same spot.

Lastly, don't dwell on the past and focus on the future instead. Practice this technique for 30 days and witness the change in your mindset.

Step 5: Strengthen Connections and Social Support

Your support system is vital since it influences your thoughts and actions and ultimately shapes your lifestyle. Knowing that you will always have firm support from your social group can help you overcome any fear and shortcoming, which is also one of the most effective approaches to building resilience.

Remember these key points when building social support and strengthening connections with the people in your life:

- Enhance your existing connections and seek opportunities to build new ones. Attend social events and join clubs that align with your interests. Learning through such communities attended by people from all walks of life will inspire you to achieve your goals and build a resilient mindset. At the same time, do not lose contact with your existing connections. Call them often, send text messages, or invite more optimistic people over lunch.

- Never be afraid to ask for help. Many consider this a sign of weakness or 'not being good enough to decipher it yourself.' While being self-reliant is admirable, remember that seeking help is only admitting that you are not perfect and need help from a supportive or experienced person. It will foster a valuable relationship that can be fruitful in the long run. Psychologists claim that asking favors from someone attracts the other person towards you, as they will feel more valued. So, do not hesitate to ask for a helping hand.

- Join forces with others. If you have a firm opinion on something (art, philosophy, politics, etc.) and share the same viewpoint with many people, get in touch with them and discuss the matter. Since your thought process matches, you may end up developing valuable friendships. You need people in life with whom you can express and share opinions. We can find such people within online communities, virtual forums, or physical events (conferences, concerts, etc.).

- Reach out to others and offer help to those in need. If you see someone struggling, try to help them resolve their problem. It may not be something big for you, but it can be life-changing for the other person.

Step 6: Know your Strengths

As you learned, self-awareness is key to building resilience, and it comes from knowing your strengths and weaknesses. When you find yourself at rock bottom, these strengths (talent, skills, achievements, experience, and knowledge) will push you forward and guide you in the right direction. Failing to acknowledge them will leave them undervalued and unappreciated.

Overcome your fear of failure. Dig deeper to decipher the root of your negative experiences. Think of all the positive outcomes that could come from that experience and what you could have done differently. Acknowledge your fear and question its root cause. Gather these new insights and reframe your goals, implement your alternative plan, and prepare a backup. Find the benefits gained from past challenges and failures and learn from them.

Do not run away from uncomfortable situations; instead, try to overcome that discomfort as it is a valuable lesson in building resilience. Avoid using your strengths to compare yourself to others, as it can trigger a condescending personality trait, which is the complete opposite of resilience. Leverage your strengths to feel more confident and empowered. In parallel, polish your skills to increase your personal value. Stay curious and keep learning as much as you can. Know your weaknesses and focus on areas that need improvement.

Step 7: Locus of Control

We know that the locus of control is known as the extent to which you can control influential events in your life. Your locus of control's radius depends on your beliefs, level of positivity, and overall resilience. You may be blessed with an internal locus of control if you believe that the events in your life are under your complete control. By contrast, if you believe that none of it is in your hands and that it is the doing of external forces, you hold an external locus of control. Your level of motivation, which governs your actions, depends on the type of locus of control you possess.

It all relates to the belief in changing one's fate. If you believe that your future lies in your hands, you will change your current situation and get a desirable outcome. On the contrary, if you think that everything is predestined and your current situation is the product of external forces, you will not bother to control or change your situation. Now, while an internal locus of control seems desirable, it is not necessarily "good." However, it helps you take charge of the situation and look at it with a better perspective, directly related to building resilience.

How can one improve their locus? An internal locus of control is relatively more desirable as it averts stress and keeps you motivated. The key to developing it is by acknowledging the fact that you do have a choice. No one is stopping you from acquiring an internal locus of control. While you cannot control the uneventful happenings in your life, you can control your attitude and the way you cope with them. Second, if you feel trapped, create a list of actions that can achieve a positive outcome. Lastly, encourage self-talk and review your options with a person whose opinion and guidance you trust.

Step 8: Develop Problem-Solving Skills

Part of your strength depends on your problem-solving skills. As soon as you encounter a problematic situation in your life, your decision-making skills and problem-solving abilities can pull you out instantly. Throughout your journey, you will face many questions and problems, some of which will be life-altering. In such cases, weak problem-solving skills can lead to poor decisions, therefore taking your life down an uncertain or even dangerous path.

Look at these useful tips to improve your problem-solving skills:
- Shift your focus from the problem onto the solution. Failing to do so will invite your mind to feed on negativity, which will worsen the situation. Think of what we can do rather than what already happened.

- Ask yourself, 'Why?'—Why did this problem occur in the first place? Why am I always late? Why is my lifestyle so unhealthy? Asking these will help you dig deeper and isolate the root cause of the problem.

- Create a list of possible solutions. Once you think of every solution, go through your list, pick one that is the most practical, safe, and follows a unique approach.

- Change your objective. Thinking outside the box is another way to find an effective solution to your problems.

Step 9: Practice Self-Care

As you already know, a lack of resilience can affect your health, be it physical, mental, or emotional. If you lack resilience, one concrete way to counterbalance its effect is by practicing self-care. Make your mental, emotional, and physical health your highest priority as it will help you lead a happier and successful life.

To that end, here are a few self-care activities that you can practice regularly:

Meditation: We have previously discussed the effects of meditation and the right way to meditate to reduce stress, calm your mind, improve focus, and become resilient.

Find Joy: Experience happiness in the smallest, most banal instances. Find ways to laugh and spread joy around you.

Self-Compassion: Before you expect anyone to love you for who you are, learn to love yourself. Self-worth and compassion start on the inside. By loving yourself, you send a signal of confidence and self-sufficiency, which will attract others towards you. We should not measure self-love through a past failure or a preconceived notion about oneself; it will only lead to self-loathing, which can destroy your image. If you love yourself in every situation and resist self-sabotage, you will automatically strengthen your resilience. Believing in yourself will help you overcome every situation, and the first step is by practicing self-compassion.

Step 10: Practice Gratitude

Gratitude is a useful tool to keep you going when things are falling apart. Whether it's the loss of a job or a financial constraint, we can overcome every difficulty in life with the feeling of being grateful. Simply put, gratitude is being thankful for the things you already have and counting your blessings. If you lack gratitude, you may find yourself pointlessly comparing your skills and resources to others. This comparison will eventually make you unhappy and undermine your resilience.

Counterintuitively, we should be thankful for experiencing difficulties in life. The universe will always balance things out. You will not appreciate the power of resilience and the blessing of happy times if you have never survived difficult situations. You will learn the true essence of light only after experiencing darkness. Experiencing both negative and positive emotions is necessary to lead a happy and grateful life. It will make you appreciate the things you have in life and be grateful for your existence.

The simplest way to practice gratitude is through journaling. Before you go to bed, list three things you are grateful for in life. It can be the house you live in, your children, or sleeping on a full stomach. There are many things to be grateful for; all you need is to expand your perspective to realize this. Similarly, giving more to others will also help you practice mindfulness and add to your happiness. Once you develop a grateful outlook, you will approach problems with a positive mindset and seek help if needed.

CHAPTER 5

FOODS TO BOOST RESILIENCE AND REDUCE STRESS

"While positive mental states may be associated with less stress and more resilience to infection, positive well-being might also be accompanied by a healthy lifestyle." - Michael Greger

Unhealthy eating habits will not only disturb your physical health but also pave the way to stress, depression, and more. Your diet affects your physical, mental, and emotional well-being more than you imagine. This chapter will discuss the foods you must eat to boost resilience, improve your well-being, and safeguard your health.

The Effects of Poor Eating

Poor eating patterns can contribute to low resilience, both mentally and physically. When you feel stressed, it is easy to turn to high-calorie foods such as sugar and refined carbohydrates to feel more energetic. However, overindulging in such unhealthy foods can cause health issues and result in weight gain. It may also subject you to other serious problems such as diabetes, high cholesterol levels, or some form of cardiovascular disease.

Factors to Consider for a Resilience-Boosting Diet

Fortify Your Brain and Nervous System: Your body's nervous system dictates your responses to stress and negative stimuli. It represents a window of tolerance that keeps you calm and stress-free. In essence, it maintains the equilibrium of your body. By staying within this tolerance window, you can perceive and process your predicament in a more positive light, a vital requisite for developing resilience. Incorporate nutritious foods such as green leafy vegetables, eggs, salmon, almonds, and avocado that promote good brain and nervous system functions.

Reduce Inflammation: If your gut experiences an imbalance of microbiota, this may cause chronic inflammation. As mentioned, we need an equilibrium to promote good body functions. Food items that can effectively treat chronic inflammation are olive oil, tomatoes, nuts, berries, and fatty fish.

Support the Immune System: The flux of gut microbiota, along with certain external stimuli, can affect immune fitness and cause imbalances, eventually leading to several health issues like allergies, development of NCDs, and chronic inflammation. Adding probiotics, prebiotic, and symbiotic ingredients in your meals can keep your immune health intact. Some of these ingredients include yogurt, kombucha, kimchi, sauerkraut, bananas, garlic, onions, oats, asparagus, barley, and apples.

Balance Blood Sugar: People with naturally high resilience can better cope with stress and anxiety than those with low resilience. The first group shows better glycemic control, which helps people deal with diabetes. If you suffer from low resilience, you may experience severe fluctuations in blood sugar levels. To keep your blood sugar level under control, work towards building your resilience. You should incorporate raw vegetables, fiber-rich food, berries, fatty fish, and eggs into your diet to balance blood sugar levels.

Five Key Nutritional Food Groups

Wholesome and balanced nutrition will boost your immune health, influence the good bacteria that govern your gut health, and reduce inflammation. These five nutritional food groups will help ease high stress, boost resilience, and keep you healthy.

1. **Vitamin B Complex:** Made of 8 types of B vitamins, the vitamin B group helps maintain your physical and mental well-being. These building blocks are responsible for cell metabolism, healthy eyesight, digestion, appetite control, cardiovascular health, and muscle toning. It would help if you had vitamin B complex to maintain equilibrium in your body, which will boost resilience. Some food items rich in vitamin B complex include eggs, milk, cheese, whole grains, soy products, fish, nuts, dark green vegetables, and seeds.

2. **Omega-3:** This group of fatty acids boosts body and brain health, reduces anxiety, protects from various heart diseases, and improves eyesight. It is necessary to increase resilience thanks to its ability to control stress. Some food items rich in Omega-3 fatty acids include salmon, olive oil, egg yolks, nuts, seeds, and avocados.

3. **Magnesium:** It is known for fighting depression, reducing stress levels, and boosting physical performance. Incorporate this vital mineral into your diet when building resilience. Some food items rich in magnesium include whole grains, nuts, low-fat dairy products, dry beans, and seeds.

4. **Vitamins C and D:** Together, these vitamins boost immune health and detoxify the body by flushing out harmful radicals that cause imbalances. Some food items rich in vitamins C and D include citrus fruits, tomatoes, broccoli, potatoes, bell peppers, winter squash, and green leafy vegetables.

5. **Antioxidants:** As mentioned, antioxidants detoxify the body and enable it to ward off harmful diseases. Furthermore, these natural compounds reduce inflammation in the body, balance normal functions, and reduce the chance of developing certain forms of cancer. Some food items rich in antioxidants are

berries, green tea, dark chocolate, goji berries, kale, pecans, and artichokes.

The Importance of Staying Hydrated

Lastly, drink enough water to stay hydrated. Proper hydration regulates your body temperature, delivers nutrients to every cell, maintains integration of organs and relevant functions, and prevents infections. Staying hydrated also enhances your sleep quality and keeps you in a good mood while reducing stress levels. It improves your skin and aids in weight loss, which adds benefits. Drink at least 8 to 10 glasses of water throughout the day for optimum hydration.

CHAPTER 6

CELEBRATING SUCCESS

"The more you praise and celebrate your life, the more there is in life to celebrate." - Oprah Winfrey

Another way to build your resilience is by celebrating your achievements, no matter how small they may be. While focusing on your primary goal should be your priority, celebrating your success will boost your confidence and grant you the courage to overcome your next objective. Consider it a necessity to elevate your resilience.

Recall the importance of knowing your strengths discussed earlier. Celebrating minor achievements will make you realize that you are capable and worthy enough to achieve bigger goals. Successful business people attribute their progress to celebrating minor goals and taking it one step at a time. Do not confuse positive affirmations with celebrating success. While the former refers to getting up every day and practicing self-talk to boost productivity, the latter entails arranging a small gathering and celebrating your milestone with your peers and loved ones. For instance, if you lead a team, gather your team members, and celebrate the success by highlighting each member's professional contribution and potential.

Nevertheless, do celebrate modestly. There is a fine line between learning from your achievements and being overconfident. One way to overcome this is by celebrating with others and highlighting everyone's progress. If you work individually, celebrate it with your family and close friends.

Once you build resilience or reconnect with your old resilient self, you will notice the following characteristics:

Faith: Ultimately, resilience is all about holding on to hope and praying that things will turn in your favor. By following a moral compass and keeping the faith, you build resilience and believe that things will get better.

Optimism and a Positive Attitude: Developing resilience without having a positive attitude is impossible. Optimistic people can survive shipwrecks and get back on their feet in no time. Both these traits go hand in hand; you cannot be resilient without a positive attitude, and vice versa. By developing an optimistic approach, you will feel and become happier. Eventually, you will inspire people to stay optimistic and maintain a positive outlook on life.

Inspiration: As mentioned, you will stay inspired in every situation and inspire those around you. It is helpful when building confidence and enhancing productivity. You will have a role model to rely on and from whom to seek inspiration. By learning about a person who has been in a similar situation, you can cling on to hope and use this inspiration as action learning.

A Sense of Humor: One of the most apparent and likable characteristics that a resilient person has is an excellent sense of humor. The ability to laugh and make others chuckle is a unique quality, something that comes with high resilience. You are open to jokes and can laugh at yourself, which is very uplifting and liberating. You will also be able to reframe a difficult situation and look at it from a fresh perspective.

Responsibility: You will notice a spike in your sense of responsibility. Whether it's work, personal relationships, or self-care, you will take responsibility and change every major aspect of your life.

Social Support: When you are positive and spread positive vibes around you, you attract more people and establish valuable connections, some of which will last a lifetime. If you have a supportive social group, including friends, family, and well-wishers, you will stay happier and carefree. Whether it's emotional, physical, financial, or mental, you can endure almost every situation in life by having a strong support network.

In the end, building resilience is all about celebrating success, as it is an arduous journey to go through. Once you build a strong resilience, you will have another reason to celebrate!

CONCLUSION

Success comes after a series of failures, and most successful people have failed multiple times at one point in their lives. However, they overcame every obstacle and hardship by being resilient, which is the key to happiness, contentment, and success. By building resilience, you can live life to the fullest and get closer to your goals. You are tougher than you think and capable of surviving any obstacle. Do not let a bad day dictate the course of your life; see it as a valuable lesson and move on.

While this book explains the what's and why's, you must pick your own battle to endure the how's. Leading a quality life is everyone's dream, and the first step to achieve that is by developing your resilience. As Dracula author, Bram Stoker once said, "It is really wonderful how much resilience there is in human nature. Let any obstructing cause, no matter what, be removed in any way, even by death, and we fly back to first principles of hope and enjoyment."

As you learned, happiness, success, self-acceptance, confidence, productivity, focus, peace, and self-esteem are all tied together by resilience. You cannot build resilience overnight; it may take a few months, years, or even a decade or two. Take it one step at a time, be consistent, and be grateful for all your achievements and hardships.

Thank you for purchasing this book. I hope you liked reading it as much as I wanted to write it. If you found the book valuable, would you consider leaving a review on Amazon? Even only a few words would assist others in deciding if the book is right for them.

Thank you in advance.

ABOUT THE AUTHOR

Inessa Scott is a self-publishing author whose interests include happiness, positive thinking, resilience, and mental toughness.

After two decades in the corporate world as a business analyst and writing business and market reports, she left to become a stay-at-home mom. Inessa continues to write from home but writing about the things she loves and spending her time gardening and stock trading.

Through her writing, she hopes that she can help others grow and overcome their mental struggles to become the best version of themselves. Inessa believes that everyone has so much potential within if they only knew how to use it. Changing even one person's life is worth all the time and effort she spends writing the things she's passionate about.

BOOKS BY THE AUTHOR

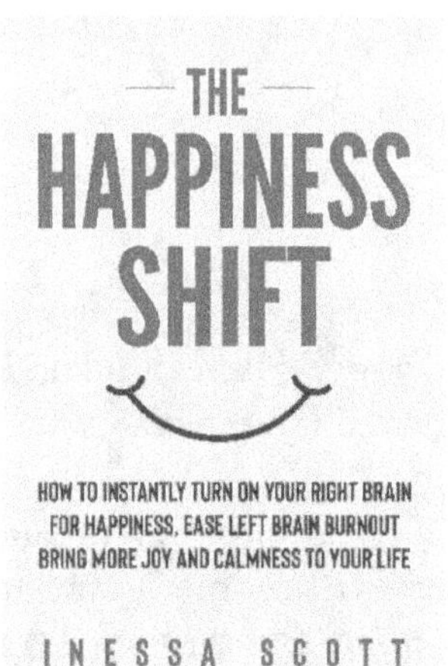

In this short-read book, you'll discover 30 simple ways to using the right brain more to control your overthinking, overcome mental burnout, and deal with anxiety in a short time.

Learn how to make the switch to the right brain to speed up the path to happiness and peace of mind. Start feeling alive now!

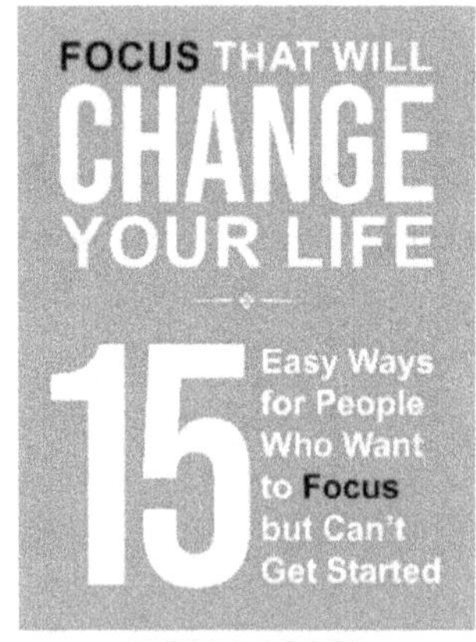

In this short book, you'll discover 15 simple ways to grow your focus a little longer each day and learn how to live your life, take control of your time, get closer to your goals but at the same time, not letting everything overwhelm you.

Learn how to focus gradually, and you will reap the rewards!